A COUPLE WITH
COMMON CENTS

"I urge you to do something special for those you love most—read this book!"

—**Dan Miller**, Author of the *New York Times* bestselling book *48 Days to the Work You Love.* 48days.com

"Over the years, I've met so many Christians who were gifted in various areas, but when it came to their finances, they lacked common sense. It's difficult bringing up the issue to such people, as money is a sensitive matter. Ryan Eidson has solved the problem for us. He has written an excellent, highly readable, modern-day parable that most North Americans can relate to. The book packs a lot of practical insight into the whole realm of finances. *A Couple with Common Cents* is a book you can happily hand to those people you want to encourage and inspire with respect to their finances."

—**Frank Viola**, Author of *Jesus Now* and *God's Favorite Place on Earth.* frankviola.org

"I mainly read self help books, not fiction. I got both here, and a bonus that has me setting new goals and rethinking my finances to make positive changes. I loved the message in this book."

—**Robin**, Early reader of the book

"I totally identified with the mom in this book. There were some good actionable tips in here."

—**Kate**, Early reader of the book

A COUPLE WITH COMMON CENTS

*A Short Story About Abundant Hope
in your Family Finances*

RYAN EIDSON

New York

A COUPLE WITH COMMON CENTS

A Short Story About Abundant Hope in your Family Finances

© 2016 RYAN EIDSON.

Published in New York, New York, by Morgan James Publishing. Morgan James and The Entrepreneurial Publisher are trademarks of Morgan James, LLC.
www.MorganJamesPublishing.com

The Morgan James Speakers Group can bring authors to your live event. For more information or to book an event visit The Morgan James Speakers Group at www.TheMorganJamesSpeakersGroup.com.

This publication is designed to provide accurate and authoritative information with regard to the subject matter covered. It is provided with the understanding that the publisher is not engaged in rendering legal, accounting, or other professional advice. If legal advice or other expert professional assistance is required, the services of a competent professional person should be sought.

A free eBook edition is available with the purchase of this print book.

CLEARLY PRINT YOUR NAME ABOVE IN UPPER CASE

Instructions to claim your free eBook edition:
1. Download the BitLit app for Android or iOS
2. Write your name in **UPPER CASE** on the line
3. Use the BitLit app to submit a photo
4. Download your eBook to any device

ISBN 978-1-63047-712-7 paperback
ISBN 978-1-63047-713-4 eBook
Library of Congress Control Number: 2015911878

Cover Design by:
Rachel Lopez
www.r2cdesign.com

Interior Design by:
Bonnie Bushman
The Whole Caboodle Graphic Design

In an effort to support local communities and raise awareness and funds, Morgan James Publishing donates a percentage of all book sales for the life of each book to Habitat for Humanity Peninsula and Greater Williamsburg.

Get involved today, visit
www.MorganJamesBuilds.com

Habitat for Humanity®
Peninsula and
Greater Williamsburg
Building Partner

In Memory of Rick Butts,

who inspired and taught me
how to write this fiction parable.

CONTENTS

Acknowledgments

Thank you to my wife, Lori, who gives me grace to try new things.

Andrew Fish, my friend, thank you for listening.

To my early readers when I first self-published this book in 2013, thanks for your feedback as I was getting close to publication.

To my team at *Macon The News*, thank you for believing in local community newspapers and helping the public discover how they missed a high-quality publication.

To those who helped bring this book to the national stage: Joel Comm, for connecting me with Morgan James Publishing; David Hancock, my publisher, for seeing more potential in this book than I did; to the entire team at Morgan James Publishing, who helped bring this book to you; to Dan Miller and Frank Viola, for your early endorsements; and to Jeff Goins, for helping me to say, "I *am* a writer."

To Jesus Christ, Who goes before and after me. You are *true* Abundance.

INTRODUCTION

You may be in a financial situation right now that you don't think you'll ever get out of.

Maybe you have a load of debt from college or a mortgage that you feel you'll never get paid off. Perhaps you're living paycheck to paycheck. Or you just want to start saving more for the future.

Whatever your circumstances, there is hope!

Through Tabitha's story in the following pages, I present a perspective of abundance that inspires you and your family to overcome the shackles of financial bondage. It's an inspirational short story set in modern-day America.

Thank you for reading. May you be blessed beyond measure!

—Ryan Eidson

Macon, Missouri

TABITHA'S STORY

Part One

THE SITUATION

"One person **gives freely, yet gains more**;
another withholds what is right,
only to come to poverty.
A generous person will prosper,
and the one who gives a drink of water
will himself be refreshed.
People will curse the one who hoards grain,
but a **blessing will come to the one who sells it**."
Proverbs 11:24-26

 # A Family of Four

Tabitha heard many birds chirping as she drove home from work. It was the first day of spring. Even though the weather was really nice outside, Tabitha had some concerns nagging at her heart.

She drove to the day care to pick up her two young children. She placed Kyle and Katie in the back seat of the family minivan. Kyle reached over to Katie and stole the toy she was playing with. She started to cry.

"It's mine and I'm playing with it!" Kyle said.

"Get along back there, you two," Tabitha said as she drove home. "Kyle, please give that back to her."

Kyle, four, loved to pester his younger sister. She just turned two the other day. He gave Katie her toy back, and she stopped crying.

Tabitha took time for reflection as she drove them home. During their first year of marriage, like most couples do, Jack and Tabitha were living high on love. They were young and did not give much thought to their long-term future. Now, nearly six years after their initial bliss, they were stuck in the grind of life.

As a handyman, Jack was truly the jack-of-all-trades. He liked to help neighbors and friends with their cars, houses, and anything that could be tinkered with. Because of his generous heart and willingness to help his friends, he often just charged them for parts and rarely billed anyone for his time. When he did, he only asked for ten dollars per hour. During business hours, Jack worked at the hardware store, so he figured that he didn't need to ask for much from the other projects he did on many evenings and weekends.

Because Jack worked so many hours, and Tabitha was better at math, he let her do all the record keeping. She prepared the invoices for his side projects—it was hardly a business, more like a hobby that generated enough income it was considered self-employment for taxes.

She balanced both of their checkbooks. For some reason, Jack was insistent that they have separate personal accounts.

She was fine with that when they wed; however, her feelings about separate bank accounts had changed since. Yet she kept to herself and had not brought up the subject with him.

Tabitha worked at a small store during the day, measuring and cutting bolts of fabric for customers. Soon after Katie was born, Tabitha and her husband, Jack, decided that two kids were enough for them. To provide for the increased expenses of a fourth member of the family, along with a new minivan and larger house, they agreed that Tab would also work a day job. This meant that someone else would watch Kyle and Katie during the day.

With no family members close by, and all their neighbors also gone from home during the day, they had few options for day care. The two ladies that watched their children were nice, but Tabitha wished that somehow Jack would earn enough so she could stay at home with the kids. Their money was so tight that neither of them could afford to miss work.

As she opened the mailbox, Tabitha looked to see what bills had arrived that day. Tossing the pile of mail into the empty passenger's seat, she told the kids, "We're home!" and pulled into the driveway. "Let's play outside for a while," she said.

Despite her weariness of standing on her feet all day, Tabitha still enjoyed chasing her kids in the yard. They all laughed when the kids chased her around, too. For a few brief moments, she did not worry about their tight financial situation.

 # INVITATION

T hat Sunday evening, Tabitha's cell phone rang.
   "Hey Tab, what's going on?"
"Just spending some time with the family at home before another long work week," Tabitha replied.

It was Linda on the other end. Linda and Tabitha were good friends ever since Tabitha came to town. Linda was one of her few friends here, as Tabitha was no longer living where she grew up. Even though Tabitha had lived here for six years now, she still felt like an outsider in the small Midwestern city of Maplewood.

Linda said, "There is a women's conference that is coming up very soon. Would you like to go with me? We can have a lot of fun together!"

Tabitha walked into the quiet bedroom so she could hear Linda better. "Where is it? And how long is this conference?"

"It's three days in Omaha, April 27-29. There will be hundreds of other ladies there. You will only spend two nights away from your family. Come on, it will be fun!"

"Oh, I can't go! I don't want to be gone from my kids that long." Tab had spent only one night away from her children since Kyle was born.

"Yes you can! Tell Jack to watch them."

"Jack works most Saturdays, you know, and often Friday late and sometimes even Sunday afternoons. How can I pull that off?"

"Oh, just go ask him," Linda replied. "You deserve some time off."

"I've never attended anything like this. What will it cost?"

Linda paused for a moment, then said, "We will split room costs between four of us. The hotel includes breakfast. We will pack Friday supper and Saturday lunch so we only have to eat out Saturday night and Sunday noon. And we won't eat at any fancy places. Registration right now is only $29, so you could go for around 70 bucks."

"Seventy dollars!" Then Tab lowered her voice, "I don't have that kind of money sitting around to be gone all weekend!"

"Well, OK. Can you promise me you will at least think about it? This early bird registration rate lasts only until Friday, so we all need to get our tickets fast."

Tab really did not want to disappoint her friend, yet knew that this would not work out. "Well, I'll see you later. Bye."

"Bye."

"Who was that?" asked Jack as she walked back into the living room.

"Just Linda."

"What did she want?"

"Not much. She just told me of an upcoming event she's going to, and wanted me to go with her. I told her no."

"Oh," Jack said, as he continued to eat popcorn and watch TV with their kids.

# PLANS

T he next evening at supper, Jack and Tabitha told each other about the events of the day.

"Kyle apparently kissed another girl while at daycare today," Tab said.

Jack laughed. "He sure is following in his father's footsteps, going after all the girls, aren't you little buddy?" he said as he rubbed on Kyle's head. "You know, that was one of my favorite subjects in school: shop class, PE, lunch, and girls."

Tab gave him a look.

"You know, I'm just kidding," he said.

Kyle piped up, "I saw a pretty girl today!"

"Finish your peas," his mother said.

They ate for one minute in silence, then Jack said, "Oh, I almost forgot!"

"What?"

"Today me and some of the guys were talking. You know, now that spring is here, we can get outside more, go fishing, and enjoy the sun."

"Are you going on some big fishing trip?" Tab asked.

"No, not with the guys. Not all of them, anyway. I want to take Kyle and Katie."

"Fish?" Katie asked as she held up a chicken nugget.

"That is chicken, not fish. Say, 'chicken,'" Tab instructed.

"Chik'n," Katie replied.

"I want some fish, Daddy!" said Kyle. "Give me some fish!"

"Not right now, Kyle. In about a month. The almanac shows that April 27 is the next best day to go fishing, after the forecasted rain in the early part of the month."

She was excited that Jack showed this much interest in a special activity with the kids. Tab did a double-take. "Did you say April 27?"

"Yes I did, sweetheart."

"Are you sure you want to take the kids fishing?"

"Yes, it will be fine. Bob will go, so there will be two adults and two kids. Bob said he will let us borrow his gear. We will go to the lake north of town. Don't worry—we will all wear life jackets. This way, I can have some daddy time with the kids."

"Yay!" clapped Kyle. "Fishing!"

"Daddy!" squealed Katie.

"What will I do during that time?" Tab asked her husband.

"You can do whatever you want. I'm giving you some time off. You have not had a day to yourself since the kids came around. Shoot, take off Saturday, too! Mommy needs a break."

She couldn't believe her ears. Jack had just cleared the calendar for her without him knowing the details of her conversation yesterday with Linda.

"Are you sure?"

"Yes, and I'll even tell my buddies that I can't do any work for them that weekend. We will be fine. It will be fun! It may take me a few extra minutes to clean up the kids, especially after eating all the fish we catch, but we will have a good time. Plus, Katie is potty-trained now," he said with a smile.

"I like to eat fresh fish, too, babe."

"We will save a piece or two for you. Hey, didn't Linda invite you to something? When is that?"

"It's the same exact weekend, Jack."

"Perfect!" Jack stood up to get more milk for the kids.

"Wait a minute," she said.

"What? The kids' cups are empty. Do you want more milk, Kyle?"

"Yes, Daddy."

"Jack," Tabitha said, "I meant, well…can we talk this over later?"

"Sure."

With that, they finished their meal. Tabitha was astonished that her path was part-way cleared.

Now she just wondered how to pay for the conference.

 # No Dinero

After they settled into bed that night, Tabitha wanted to continue her conversation with Jack. "Babe? I need to tell you something."

"What is it?" Jack said as he yawned.

"We don't have the money for me to go to the conference with Linda."

"Yes, we do. Surely we have enough. We always have enough to do what we need to do, don't we?"

"No, Jack, I'm afraid this time we don't."

"How much does it cost? It can't be that much to be gone for a weekend."

"If I register right now, pack some food, and spend some to share a room and eat out a couple times, Linda estimated the cost at about seventy dollars."

"Shoot, seventy bucks. I probably have that in my wallet."

"I just checked an hour ago. You only have twelve dollars in your wallet."

Jack raised his voice. "You're telling me we don't have seventy dollars of cash between all four of us right now?"

"We don't."

"Since when have we been out of money?"

"For a long time, Jack." Tabitha started to get nervous, like she always does when this topic comes up.

"I don't want to talk about this any more tonight. We need to get to sleep so we can work tomorrow and make more money, because apparently we don't have any."

With that, Jack fell asleep as Tab shed some quiet tears on her pillow.

FAST CASH

T he issue of money was on her mind all throughout the next day at work.

When she took her lunch break and ate her homemade sandwich, a thought came to her: she only needed $29 by Friday for the early registration fee, and she had until the day of the conference to come up with the rest of what she needed.

Just then, a coworker came to the break room and asked Tabitha if she would watch two kids that night. She offered $30.

"Yes! Yes, I can do that," Tab said.

As soon as her coworker walked out the door, Tab called Linda and said that she could go. They were both excited!

Tab didn't have to worry about the remaining conference money for long. Other people were looking for sitters, too, because a couple neighborhood teens who had watched children were no longer reliable. The word got out that Tab wanted to watch other families' children one evening each week.

Kyle and Katie loved having other kids to play with at their house.

Tab enjoyed cooking for more people, and really appreciated the extra income.

Jack didn't mind it, as long as the children behaved and the other kids went home in a timely manner.

Tab prepared for her departure the best that she could. She had everything ready for herself, Jack, and the kids. She had enough spending money and even saved some back for later.

Part Two

THE CONFERENCE

"Salvation destroys the law of sin and death and introduces the economy of life, in which there is **no end of resources.** *"*

—Dr. Paul V. Axton

HANNAH

The women's conference was in a large convention center. Tab walked into the arena that seated several thousand people, and felt much energy and excitement around her. She felt somewhat out of place because she had never attended an event this large before.

Tab was not impressed with the main session. It was too much hype for her. She felt like it was an over-produced everybody-feel-good session. All she knew was: if the entire weekend was going to be like that, she felt like it was a waste of her money and time.

After the first session concluded, all the women quickly browsed through their program books to pick which workshop to attend. Unlike the rest of the group she traveled with, Tab knew none of the speakers presenting that weekend, so she could not pick a workshop based on name recognition.

Some of the ladies, including Linda, attempted to persuade Tab to stick with them for all the workshops.

"The speaker from last hour has an entire workshop track this weekend to herself," Linda said. "I've read her books before, and they are so good! She has one of the most popular blogs for women these days. Why don't you come with us, Tab?"

"I want to go to a workshop that will benefit my family," Tab replied. "I'll stick with you for the main sessions. For now, I need a few more minutes to pick."

"Well, a few minutes is all you've got. Classes start in ten minutes. See you later."

Tab went to the restroom for a quick break. She turned on the faucet to wash her hands and encountered a friendly lady at the sink.

"Hi! How are you today? My name's Hannah, what's yours?"

"Tabitha Cundiff, but you can call me Tab."

"Do you have a workshop picked out that you're going to?"

"Um, not yet. I don't, actually."

"Are you looking for something in particular?" Hannah asked.

"I'd like to attend one that will help my family. I'm not going to one just because 'everyone else is doing it,' like the rest of the group I came with."

"What would help your family the most right now, then?"

"Finances. We're really tight on our budget right now. It's amazing that I even had the money to come this weekend."

"I know the perfect one for you," Hannah said. "It was a last-minute addition to the program, so it didn't get printed in the program book. I first read her work online six months ago. When she announced her upcoming presentation here in Omaha, I knew I had to come. Let's go meet her."

"Great! What's her name?"

"Ruth."

RUTH

The moment Tab and Hannah walked into the small conference room for their first workshop of the weekend, they knew this was the one for them.

Ruth's salt-and-pepper hair, as well as the large family photo on display with children and grandchildren, exhibited her wisdom even before she began to speak to the group.

"Good afternoon, ladies! I trust you're having a wonderful day. My name is Ruth. I'm affectionately known as 'Grandma' to the eight small children you see in this photo. We are a family full of love, far from perfect, yet we have learned many lessons along the way. I'd like to share some of those lessons with you this weekend.

"Before we go any further, I'd like to hear from each of you. I have a couple rules to guide our discussions: we will look for the good in each situation, we will not gossip about husbands or friends, and we will respectfully listen to each others' stories. Agreed?"

"Yes," replied all the participants. A few who neglected to turn their cell phones off proceeded to do so without prompting from Ruth.

There were a total of fifteen ladies in the room, including Ruth, Hannah, and Tabitha. Because of her teaching style, and the size of the group, Ruth had each lady share a thirty-second snapshot of themselves.

Here's what Tabitha said: "My name is Tabitha, I'm married with two young children. My husband and I each have jobs outside the home. I want to see our finances in better condition than they are now."

"Thank you, Tabitha," Ruth said. "I appreciate you staying positive."

After each lady briefly introduced herself, and Ruth shared a little more of her story, she went to the topic at hand.

"I understand that each one of you wants some type of financial freedom. Earlier I heard several of you mention that you want out of debt, help with your budget, or the flexibility to live out your dreams. Tell me more about how you feel about these things."

Everyone lively participated in the discussion:

"I feel like I'm working for the bank each month when I write checks for the car loan and mortgage."

"I wish that I didn't have to keep paying on a student loan for a degree I'm no longer using."

"I hate it when I have to give up buying a new dress just so my children can have new school supplies and clothes every August."

"I wish that I could talk with my husband about our money, and our lives, without being afraid of the response he may give."

"I loved it when we were first married and had extra money in savings. Now, we're living paycheck to paycheck."

Ruth asked another great question: "Does it have to be that way?"

"Yes, it seems like whatever we try to do, we can't seem to get out of the mess we're in," was the general consensus of the group.

"You're telling me you've tried everything under the sun in an attempt to change?" Ruth probed. "Exactly what have you done? Not what you tried to do, but what activities did you engage in to create the change you want to see?"

The group came up with quite a list that Ruth wrote on a flip chart:

- Date nights
- Counseling
- Motivational seminars
- Personal finance books
- Secretly hide cash
- Work longer or take a second job

Tabitha totally resonated with many items on this list. She felt very comfortable knowing that this discussion was profitable, and not just a gripe session like she observed everywhere else.

Ruth took the conversation further, "Why is it, ladies, that these things you have tried to do, don't work?"

The conversation continued to flow:

"I feel that when I try to move my family forward in the area of our money, my husband's not totally on board. He gives verbal affirmation, yet it's so hard for all of us to do what needs to be done."

"As a single mom of three, I've tried everything I know to do, and I've given up on trying to change anything. I've just learned to live in the situation I'm in and I'm doing the best I can with what I've got."

"The motivation wears off so quickly. Then I put off my record keeping because, well…I'm afraid to confront the reality once more."

"I'm just not so sure that I can get my husband and children all on the same page again. It's hard to be the role model in money when it seems like I'm the only person I know in town who is trying to make these changes."

Ruth made a few notes on the board. "Anything else?"

"Yeah, I've got something," one of the younger ones said. "I'm too busy. Like too busy with all the day-to-day to change anything. Plus, my family likes the routine we're in and I don't think they want to change. Or, at least, that's what I think."

"I don't want to be the one to upset the fruit basket!" Everyone laughed.

"I love my husband, I mean, I really do, and my kids, and I want to do what's best for all of us. I'm just so frustrated that everything I've tried so far hasn't worked," Hannah said.

"Has it worked a little, or just not to your ideal?" Ruth asked.

"Well, it worked for a little while, I guess."

"What part? When specifically, did you start to see change?"

Hannah replied, "When I took an active interest in my husband. I asked him more questions, found out what he wants to do, and I did those things with him. Even though I could care less about golf, or reading the latest business book, I caddied a couple days of golf for him and asked him what he learns from his reading. The benefit is not that I now know the difference between a driver and putter, but that he lights up and does a better job with the house and kids when I'm genuinely interested in him."

"Did you catch that, ladies?" Ruth asked the rest of the group. Everyone nodded. "Let's do some role-playing now. We will partner up to practice our communication skills and learn to have genuine interest in the other person. Here's how it will work…"

The rest of the hour, the ladies practiced their communication skills with each other as Ruth taught them. When they finished, Ruth prayed for the families represented in the room.

Tab could hardly wait for the second workshop on the next day. She made a new friend with Hannah, too, and they exchanged numbers. "See you tomorrow!"

"Yes, looking forward to it."

 ABUNDANCE

W elcome to our second of three sessions in our workshop series on mastering your money. In my experience as a wife, mother, and grandmother, and discussions with hundreds of women just like you, I've found a major hiccup in the thought process of most people."

Tab and Hannah listened closely with the other participants.

Ruth continued, "Due mainly to the influence of our schools, media, and culture at large, we've been led to believe that there's not enough to go around. Not enough oil for our energy and transportation needs. Not enough food for each person on the planet. Not enough channels to watch on TV (and not enough TVs in our homes). Not enough teachers in our schools. Not enough jobs for the unemployed. I could go on, but I think you're clearly reminded through these examples that most people talk and think about scarcity all day long.

"We've been led to believe that everything is in short supply. However, I do not believe that."

Tabitha leaned forward.

"I believe there are plenty of resources to go around. I think the planet is capable of producing food for many more people, there are enough jobs to go around, plenty of opportunities for creating new work, and adequate energy to drive our vehicles and heat our homes.

"Ladies, when is the last time you truly went without?"

Everyone stopped to think for a moment.

"Have you ever missed an entire day of eating because you were too broke to buy some vegetables? Have you ever been without a reliable supply of clean water to drink? Have you ever froze to death because you lacked shelter and heat during a blizzard? Obviously not, because you're with us today."

A few women quietly laughed at her last statement.

"Look at our society as a whole. Many people spend money on cable or satellite TV, lottery tickets, and other forms of entertainment, then complain that their kids are starving and are doing poorly in school. They expect someone or something else, such as the government, to fix their personal problems. I just don't understand.

"Ladies, I believe when we get our priorities straightened out, and our lives align with the Truth, is when we understand what is at the very core of the universe that we live in.

"I believe that at the very core of the universe is Abundance. His name is Jesus. He is full of love and He freely gives away His love. He gives of Himself, actually. And for those of us who walk in His path, He is Abundant Life.

"He drives out the fear, and fills your life to the brim, even overflowing.

"Ladies, we have more than enough, don't we?"

"Yes!" they replied.

"We may get frustrated with our families and our coworkers some days. And we can be thankful that we have families who love us and jobs that generate income. We have lives of meaning as we live in His abundance and serve others. We have more than enough. Ladies, we are truly blessed beyond measure when we open our eyes to see reality."

Tabitha wrote in her notebook, I am blessed beyond measure.

The group had a few minutes of discussion, took a short break, then resumed class.

 # THE COOKIE JAR

W e've established the foundation of our new understanding as abundance," Ruth said as the group reconvened, "not scarcity. In a world of scarcity, we fight and claw for what we think we deserve. In a world of abundance, which is the world I live in, we hold our hands open as we gratefully accept what we have, and are generous with others as well.

"Now, I do realize that you can't give away all of your money, because you need some to sustain your household. You need to take care of your family first. You can't give away 100% of your time because without rest, you will burn out and have nothing left to give. You do need to have clear boundaries in your life.

At the same time, you can still experience the abundance all around you.

"Where do we go next after laying the foundation of abundance? I like to illustrate the next part with something I know you are all familiar with: cookies!"

Suddenly, two waiters appeared and brought in platters of gooey, fresh-baked cookies. Tabitha's mouth watered.

"Go ahead, have one or two," encouraged Ruth. "There's several kinds of cookies for you to sample.

"I have fond memories as a little girl helping my grandmother make cookies in her small kitchen. She used hundreds of pounds of flour and sugar all those years, and put a lot of love into her cookies as well. Grandma's cookies were always much better than the ones you can buy at today's convenience stores and supermarkets."

"Yes, I agree," said one of the participants as she licked her lips.

"Now, I'm the grandma and enjoy my grandchildren helping me make cookies. I love on them, give them cookies and milk, and some more cookies, and then…send them home!"

The whole group laughed so hard that the class next door could hear them.

"I think of it like this," continued Ruth, "the raw ingredients of the cookies: flour, butter, sugar, are the talents that I bring to the table in my work. The time I put into making the cookies, and the oven that heats them up, represent my job. You may work for someone else, or be self-employed. Either way, you do something that provides value to other people: a product, service, or both. When you pull the cookies out of the oven, you see the fruit of your labor.

"Now, who has a cookie jar in your house that you actually use for cookies?" Most of the hands went up. "Tell me, what usually happens after you let the cookies cool on the rack?"

One lady said, "I'll put all the ones not stolen off the counter into the cookie jar!" Everyone laughed again. "Before I know it, the jar is empty within a day or two. All the neighbor kids stop by and eat some with my children. My husband takes some with him to work. Then he will come home, want an easy snack, open the lid of the cookie jar, and be disappointed that there are no cookies left! So then, in my next spare moment, I make a new batch and fill up the jar again."

Many heads in the room nodded. Some let out an agreeable, "Mm-hmm."

"Are you frustrated that you have to frequently fire up your cookie factory?" asked Ruth.

"Yes, yes I am, not because my husband constantly visits the jar, but because I want to keep my whole family happy. Sometimes I wish I could give some to kids who don't have the pleasure of experiencing homemade cookies, too."

Ruth said, "Ladies, what you've just heard is a parallel to your family's finances. Many families today live paycheck to paycheck. They spend all their money, all their cookies, before the next batch goes into the jar." She held up a classic cookie jar.

"Think of this cookie jar as your checkbook. Cookies, I mean money, go in as a result of your work. Then you take money out to pay your bills, feed your family, and do the things you want to do. Then everyone's stressed out and frustrated because the cookies, your cash, run out before you have the opportunity to put more in.

"Do you feel like you're in a daily grind, running on the treadmill constantly just to make ends meet?"

Heads nodded and hands went up.

"What if it didn't have to be that way? What if you could live without the constant stress of barely meeting your obligations? What if I could show you a way to have your experience of the cookie jar match the underlying reality of abundance? Would you be interested in that?"

"Yes!" they all cried out.

"The quickest way to get out of this rut is to slow down the rate that you eat your cookies. By this I mean cutting expenses. What do you really need in order to live?"

They took a few minutes to compile a list of needs on the flip chart:

- Food
- Water
- Clothing
- House/place to live
- Car/transportation
- Basic utilities

"Spend your money first on these items which are essential to your household. Keep the lights and the water meter on. Get your groceries. Pay your rent or mortgage.

"Cut out unnecessary expenses or reduce them. Can you take your lunch to work instead of eating out? Can you make more meals at home instead of visiting the fast food drive-thru every day? Can you wear that outfit a few more times before replacing it? Do you really need to maintain subscriptions to all your digital and print entertainment?

"Let's now list some ways to generate more income. What can you do in the next thirty days to make some more money?"

They added this list to the next page of the flip chart:

- Watch kids for other couples
- Bake sale
- Garage sale
- Take on part-time job, or switch from part-time to full-time work

Ruth gave some more great advice. "Of course you could come up with hundreds more ideas than what we've listed here. You just have to make sure that the changes you make are in alignment with your goals as a couple.

"We will talk more about goals tomorrow. Back to the cookie jar model. From my experience, cookies last longer when they're out of sight and out of reach. One way to make your cookies last longer is to put some of them in the freezer for a later time."

"Kind of like a savings account," Tab said.

"Yes, you're exactly right, Tabitha!" Ruth said. "When you put money away for later, such as a savings account, you can save for larger purchases later on, have extra money for emergencies, take a vacation, and pay cash for Christmas gifts.

"Which leads me to an important point: paying cash for everything. One of the things that contribute to financial messes is debt. Debt puts you in bondage. Who really wants to go to work all their life just to pay off the house, cars, and credit cards? What fun is it to always be a slave to other people? I know that some families have now experienced debt for generations, and you may not agree with me on this topic. For now, I'll just say that the day my husband and I paid off our last debt, our mortgage, it felt like a big relief to both of us. We were free from the chains of debt! That nagging feeling of oppression was gone! My husband could truly relax like he'd never done before.

"Now, with your cookie jars, you have money you're using today, and money you're saving back for later. You may already have some form of long-term savings, too, such as a 401(k) or an IRA.

"That leaves us with the last part: giving freshly baked cookies away. When you wait until later to give some away, you're less likely to do so. The jar may be empty when a neighbor comes by, needs some cookies, and you have none left to give! I say, in advance, while you're making the cookies, decide how much to give away. Put some aside in a bag or foil so your kids don't accidentally use what's not intended for them. In fact, you can use the cookie giving as a great lesson on generosity for your children. You can show them how to be generous with their own cookies, too.

"We have one session left. Before you go, pair up with a partner or group of three and pray for each others' families. Take five minutes to do so, then you may be dismissed."

Tabitha and Hannah prayed for each others' husbands and children, that their hearts would be softened and eyes opened to the possible changes that may be forthcoming for their families. They prayed for open, clear communication and gentle understanding when they arrived home. They also prayed for practical ways to show love to their husbands and children.

 # FORWARD THINKING

T abitha's attitude about the conference was much better now than after the first main session. All the women enjoyed it in their own way: some just took a break from family, others went to spend time with girlfriends. Tab had her own purpose for attending. She soaked up as much wisdom and encouragement as she could during the weekend, and wanted to take as much home to her family as possible. Her only worry was: how will her husband receive her new ideas? Will she continue in despair or see some real change?

Tab looked over her notes again as she walked into the conference room for the final workshop with Ruth. When she took a seat by her new friend Hannah, Ruth began their final class by saying, "Some of you spoke with me after our second workshop about the concerns you have moving forward. I know how difficult it is for you right now, because you want to quickly see change happen, yet you also know the reality of what your household is like now. It's easy to get on an emotional high at events like this and have all your new ideas fizzle out within a week after you arrive back home.

"In order to carry your momentum forward, we're going to complete a few exercises together. These are easy enough for you to do with your families as well. The key is for you to take the initiative to start these discussions at home. Get your pen and paper out. Ready?

"First, take five to ten minutes to write down everything you are thankful for. Remember ladies, we are blessed beyond measure."

All of them, even Ruth, made long lists.

"Now, what do you want your finances to look like? Describe your ideal situation. Do you want to be out of debt? Be financially independent? Have x amount in an emergency or opportunity fund? Work less hours? Write what comes to mind. You have five minutes."

Each woman wrote down her perfect financial future.

"Now, we have to face the facts. How are things right now with your money? Be totally honest. From your perspective, how's your household finances right now? Write it down."

They wrote down all of what they said at the beginning of the first workshop, and more.

Ruth stood back up in the middle of the circle. "Now that you can clearly see where you want to go, and where you are now, what are the next steps for you to take in this journey? Number one should be, 'Talk with…'"

"My husband," all the married ones replied.

"You may need to devote more time to your record keeping, budget, and analysis. Maybe eat out less. Maybe get all your credit cards paid off. Whatever they are, list specific things you can do this month, even this week, to take you in the direction you want to go. I'll give you a little more time on this one."

Everyone wrote down clear action steps to take.

Ruth then reviewed everything they discussed over the entire weekend. "Now the hard part is following through with the action plan you just wrote down. There are plenty of resources in print and online to help you in specific areas of personal finance by some great authors.

"What you really need for long-term success is a support system. This means real people for encouragement in your journey. This may be tough since none of us live in the same city as another person here.

"In addition, my husband and I offer financial coaching for families. If you are married, you will both need to agree to do it, for we're not going to get on a conference call with just one of you. In this handout I list the details of the financial coaching and other resources by me and other people.

"I'd also suggest that you get the contact information of your prayer partners from this group. That way you can actually call and check in with each other and make it more meaningful and honest than what usually happens over email or social media. Can we commit to that?"

"Yes," they said.

"Go ahead and exchange info now, and I'll answer any questions you have for me or the group before we go."

After they wrapped up, Tab approached Ruth privately to thank her for her wisdom and instruction.

"You're very welcome, Tabitha," she replied. "It was a pleasure to meet you."

 # FALLING INTEREST RATES

T abitha was all excited and tired at the same time. She already missed Ruth and Hannah, and all that they experienced together. Now it was Sunday, and Tab was going home with the other ladies in the van.

Linda said, "Tab, you seem different today than you did on Friday. Is something wrong?"

"No, not really."

"Are you sure?"

"Well, I am excited to see my family. But my heart is just so heavy with all the changes I want to see happen."

"What changes?"

Tab wasn't sure whether to tell her or not, with the possibility of the others in the van listening in. "My husband and I really need to change the way we handle our money. Things have been so tight. I told you when you first asked me to come to this conference that I didn't have the money to come, remember?"

"Yes, and…?"

"And I worked extra to get the cash to pay for this."

"Cash? I just charged the entire weekend to my credit card. I'll eventually get it paid off. I just wanted to have a good time," said Linda. "Didn't you have a good time, Tab?"

"It was a nice break from my routine. It was nice to be gone for a change. However, I didn't just come for a good time. I came to learn something. And I plan on doing something about what I've learned."

"Oh come on, you know that all husbands get stuck in a rut and don't want to change. They are in their own little world. I do what I need to do, my husband does his thing, and we go from there. What makes you think you can just go home from a conference and change everything in your little world at home?"

Tab's heart deflated quickly as those words pierced her new dreams. She decided not to say any more to Linda about this because of all the discouragement she just received.

She had a long rest of the ride back home.

Part Three

CHOICES AND CHANGES

"Every time you give, you make a statement of personal power and autonomy: 'I am not a slave to money. Money is my slave. **I believe I will always have enough**, *and more is coming my way.'"*
—**Perry Marshall**, *80/20 Sales and Marketing*, p. 191

 # HOME

B riskly walking up the stairs to her family's front door, Tab yelled, "I'm home!" The door opened with excitement as her husband and children all crowded around her.

"I missed you," each of them said to her as they exchanged kisses.

"Something smells good," Tab said as she walked into the kitchen. "Looks like you caught some fish and saved some back for me!"

"Yeah, we had a great time, didn't we?" Jack asked the kids.

"Mommy, I caught a fish and it was this big!" Kyle said, holding his hands as far apart as they would go. "It was so big that all of us ate from that one fish and we all got full."

"Sounds like we have a storyteller in our midst," Tab said, as she gave Jack a wink.

She was sure glad to see her family, and quickly composed her response to the inevitable questions about her trip.

"How was the conference?"

"Good. There were hundreds of women there. And I made a few new friends, too."

"Wow, how did you meet?"

"We went to the same workshop. I didn't know which one to attend at first, but met one new friend who helped me pick one out. Hannah is her name. When she said that the topic was on..."

At this point, Tab didn't think Jack was listening to her. The kids chased each other around the house and Jack made sure they were not making a big mess of the house. Tab turned around to make sure the meal prep continued unhindered, for all the fishermen had abandoned camp.

 SPARE CHANGE

T abitha went back to work the next day as her family resumed their weekly routine: parents working and other people watching their children. Oh, how she wanted to be home with her kids!

Tab served many customers throughout the morning. Then, out of the blue, Linda walked in.

"Hi, Linda, what brings you here today?"

"Oh, just taking an early lunch. Did you tell Jack all of your juicy new ideas?"

"What?"

"Did you tell Jack how you want everything to change at home?"

"Our marriage is none of your business, and you don't need to pry into what we have or have not talked about."

"Well, sorry!" exclaimed Linda. "I was just seeing how things were going."

"I don't appreciate the way you have talked to me recently," Tab said as she looked at Linda. Linda's eyes were downcast.

"Oh, look at the time, I had better keep on moving. I need to go do something else," Linda said as she hurried out of the store.

Tab felt that her friend was not really in support of how she wanted to improve her family's situation. Had she lost a friend?

 # Date Night Disaster

D ebt will *always* be part of life!" Jack said as he dropped his fork on his plate. Some of the people at adjacent tables in the restaurant gave Jack a look because he had raised his voice.

Tab looked down at her plate. She knew this date night dinner did not get off to a good start.

Jack lowered his voice and continued, "I have seen debt my whole life, and I'm used to it. My father has always carried an operating loan on his farm so that he could keep the farm running in order to feed us.

"So you're telling me that you want to change what we've done all these years just because of what one woman said at the conference last weekend?"

"Jack, listen to me. I've tried to tell you for several months about our lack of funds. What I saw last weekend were several other families in the same situation as us, and the hope that it doesn't have to continue being like this."

"I don't see any reason to change what we're doing. We have a place to live, there's plenty of food to eat, and our kids seem to be happy. I'm happy. So there."

"Jack, what if I told you that I'm not happy with the situation? Maybe I need to sit down with you and show you the whole picture. I need to show you where we are headed."

"Tabitha, do I have money in my wallet?"

"Yes, last time I checked, you do."

"Is there gas in the car? Do we have enough to pay the sitter for tonight and for this meal?"

"Yes, but…"

"Then I think we're doing OK."

"Jack, what if you get laid off? What if the store I work for closes suddenly, or one of us gets injured and can't go to work? What if we…"

"Enough with the 'what if's,' OK? We will deal with any of that when the time comes."

They stopped talking to eat some more. Tab found that she was no longer hungry.

"Can I ask a different question, Jack?"

"I suppose."

"Let's think about the kids for a few minutes. I wish I could stay home with them now. In just a few years they will be in school. A few short years after that, each of them will have a drivers license, and before you know it, off to college."

"What about it? That's a long way off. Maybe they won't want to attend college. I didn't, and I turned out just fine."

"And maybe they will," she replied. "Don't you think we should put some money aside to help them for those things? Not that we have to buy them brand new cars or fund an Ivy League education, but just so that they have some money to use as a gift from us."

"Well, how are we supposed to do that if we are struggling to pay our own bills at the moment?" Jack asked.

"That's what I'm trying to show you, Jack, a picture of a different future for our kids."

"That's not even feasible right now, so let's not even consider it, alright?" he said.

Suddenly, her phone rang. Tab checked to see who it was. "It's the sitter. I better answer it." She usually did not pick up the phone during meals.

"Hello?"

"Tabitha, this is Bri. Listen, we need to get your son to the emergency room. Kyle had an accident."

Tab could hear her boy wailing in the background. "Jack, we need to get home fast."

"Kyle fell down on the curb outside. He cut open his forehead and says that his arm hurts really bad. I know basic first-aid, but you had better get here quick," said Bri.

"Pay the bill, Jack, we need to get home. Kyle is hurt."

 # Gratitude

The doctor walked out of the operating room. "Kyle's going to be fine. We reset his arm and put a cast on it. His forehead is OK, just need to make sure he doesn't pull on those stitches. And you can bring him back in a few weeks for us to check on his arm. My assistant will schedule that appointment for you. I'll be back in a few minutes. At that time, I'll take you in to see Kyle."

"Thank you, Dr. Beal," Tabitha said.

After a few minutes, Tab asked Jack, "How are we going to pay for all of this? Our insurance deductible is very high to keep our premiums low and save money. Now we have to come up with the money to meet our deductible. What are we going to do?" She started to sob.

Jack finally started to feel the weight of his family's situation. "There's not much we can do at the moment about that. We can take our boy home tonight. Let's be thankful that Kyle is alive and that we have good doctors here."

They took a minute to pray a prayer of gratitude, then the doctor came back. "Let's go see your son."

DAN

Jack went to work with a lot on his mind. Though he would not fully admit it to Tabitha, he did have some concerns about their finances, especially now that they had to pay for a hospital bill.

"Jack, what's wrong? You're usually happy when you come to work!" It was Dan, the hardware store owner and manager.

"My son went to the emergency room. He broke his arm."

"What happened?"

Jack told Dan the story.

"Is he OK?"

"Yes, the doctors did a great job. Just a cast on his right arm and a few stitches on his forehead. Kyle's tough. He will be fine."

"Is that all that's bothering you?"

Because they had known each other for a long time, Jack felt that he could tell the truth. "We don't know how we will pay for this bill."

"You have insurance through our carrier, right?"

"Yes, but Tab said we don't have enough to meet our deductible."

"Oh, I see. Do you have any ideas how you could come up with what you need?" Dan asked.

"I know I don't want a huge community benefit fundraiser. I think that will bring shame to me, that I couldn't provide for my family. It's hard enough just telling you about this."

"I appreciate your honesty, Jack," replied Dan. "I will not tell anyone else unless you give me permission, OK?"

"Thank you," said Jack.

"Come with me, let's sit down in my office for a few minutes."

After Dan shut his door, he said, "I've had my share of financial stress, as you well know. Raised three kids and sent them on their way when they moved out. Started my own business from scratch, sold it, and later bought this hardware store. I've helped many people over the years. Through this store, I have provided excellent materials to hundreds, even thousands, of families, and have provided jobs for several people, including yourself.

"During my life I've met some wise people who helped me at just the right time. When I come to a fork in the road, I seek out wise counsel from others, because I know that those critical decisions affect the trajectory of my life and business.

"There is one wise person I see so often that it's easy to ignore her. Yes, I'm talking about my wife, Julie. She has intuition and discernment at times that just blows me away. Jack, even though you don't see her in the day-to-day operations of this store, Julie has been, and continues to be, critical in my success.

"I say all of this because I want to make sure you are openly listening to your wife. You said earlier Tab told you that you don't have enough cash to pay for the deductible, right?"

"Yes, she said that," Jack replied.

"Does she take care of all the finances at home?"

"Yes, she does. She even does the paperwork for my handyman jobs, too."

"Jack, tell me more about what you said earlier, you want to 'provide for my family.' What does that mean to you?"

Jack immediately said, "I provide for my family by working jobs that give us income to pay our obligations."

"Anything else?"

"Yes. I fix anything in our house that needs fixing, such as a slow drain, or a burned-out bulb, things like that."

"Would you consider that providing for your family also includes watching your finances to ensure there's no 'slow drain' that could make you go broke?"

"Oh, I'm no good at math. That's why Tabitha does all of that."

"Has she ever invited you into the conversation? Has she explained your family finances to you before you went to the ER?"

"Yes, but I always tell her that I want to talk about it later."

"Jack, I'm going to be straight with you. 'Later' and 'someday' are today. You're at a crossroads right now in your family's life, where you can continue to do the same thing you've always done, or you can go down the other path so you don't have to be embarrassed about not having enough money to pay your obligations. Which will it be, Jack? This is a choice that you and Tab need to make together."

"I want to make sure we have enough so that Tabitha is not worried about it."

"How much is 'enough,' Jack?"

"Hmm…"

"Don't give me that answer, this is something that you and your wife need to talk about. You know, that's what I heard another wise lady say a while back. She observed that money issues are a symptom, not the cause, of the majority of marital issues. Ruth's observation was that communication comes first."

"Who did you say said that?"

"Ruth. She is a well-known financial expert to businesspeople like me. Do you know her?"

"I think I ought to."

DISCUSSION

Jack went home with renewed enthusiasm. Tab could tell. "You must've had a good day at work today," she said.

"Yes, I did. A lot of customers came in, and I had a good talk with Dan. Sit down, babe, I want to hear your conference story again."

"You want to hear the whole story? The entire weekend? Why?"

"Just tell me the whole thing. I'm not sure I listened to the entire story in the first place."

Tab recalled everything that happened during her trip to Omaha. She told him of all that happened in the van rides, the first main session, meeting Hannah, the workshop series with Ruth, and all the meals she had.

"That must be the same Ruth that Dan knows," Jack said.

"Dan knows Ruth?"

"Apparently she's well-known in small business circles as someone who knows her stuff."

"Yes, she does," replied Tab, "and she gave us ladies a few ideas for discussion to have with our husbands. But from what I felt the other night at the restaurant before Kyle broke his arm, you weren't ready to talk about these things yet."

"I'm willing to talk about whatever you want to talk about. No more saying, 'someday' about our finances, because 'someday' never comes."

"Could you help me fix supper and talk with me at the same time?" she politely asked.

"Sure. What are we having tonight?"

As they walked into the kitchen together, for the first time they discussed their ideal financial situation as a family, as each one of them saw it. They had some differences, of course, and came to an agreement on some key points. Then they defined their current reality, as per Tabitha's accurate record keeping. After supper, they discussed concrete ways of making progress toward their long-term goals, starting that night. Tabitha took notes of everything they agreed on.

"I never realized how bad of shape we were in until Kyle broke his arm," Jack told her. "I know you've tried to tell me several times, babe, but I just would not listen. I'm sorry."

"I forgive you, Jack," she said. "I'm glad we could talk all of this through. There's one major component left, though."

"What's that?"

"We need other people, a support system, to help us move in this direction and stay firm to our commitments. It's not going to be easy, you know."

"Yeah, I'm already starting to miss all my TV shows, and I haven't even called the cable company and video streaming service to cancel yet. I'll do that first thing in the morning after we eat breakfast."

"Thanks, babe. I love you."

"I love you too."

THE BOTTOM LINE

Their support system, though not ideally all local, was now in place. They contacted Ruth to begin their financial coaching sessions. Tab called Hannah and they gave each other a status report. Jack gave Dan permission to ask him at random times how they were doing in communication and finances. Dan even gave Jack his Christmas bonus early to help the family pay the hospital and doctor bills for Kyle.

Jack began to charge all his customers a labor fee, instead of just some of them. He even raised his rates. Now his business became more consistent each month. Tabitha resumed watching other children one night a week, and they all worked diligently to cut expenses and save back an emergency fund.

However, the bottom line was not quite working the way they wanted it to.

"I think we need to sell this house and get a smaller one," Tab said to Jack one day.

"A smaller house! You know how much work we've put into this house! And how hard would it be to find another place that we would like?"

"Jack, just please look at this with me. At the current rate, we're still going to pay on this place after the kids move out. After we sold all our extra stuff the past couple months, I now see that we have too much unused space here. Since we don't need this much house anymore just to hold all our stuff, and we are not going to have any more kids, we could find a smaller place. We don't need a house this big. Plus, if we find the right house for a good deal, and sell this one, I could stay at home all day with the kids and open a small day care. What do you think about that?"

"Does it have to be an either-or decision, as in: either we stay here, or we move and start a day care? Couldn't you use the extra room we have here for day care purposes?"

"I guess I'd have to run the numbers. I hadn't considered that, Jack. Give me some time for projections, and then we can continue that discussion."

"Sure thing, Tab," he said.

FORGIVENESS

A couple days later, Tabitha realized that she had not talked with Linda as often as she had before. Jack realized this, too, and encouraged Tab to make amends.

After she got off work that day, Tab went to see Linda at her house.

"I know that recently it's been a little different between the two of us, and a lot different for me at home. I just want to say I'm sorry for neglecting our friendship. When you made the comments that you did right after the women's conference to me, I felt that you did not support what I was attempting to do, so I withdrew."

"Oh, thank you, Tab, for telling me that," said Linda as she reached out to hug her. "I'm sorry for the way I treated you. After I watched you actually go through the changes you wanted to make, I realized that my family and I needed to make some major financial adjustments as well. My husband has bugged me for years that we need to do something different, and now I have inspiration from you to actually do something. I forgive you. Will you help us get started with this?"

"Sure, we can help."

PENNIES
BECOME DOLLARS

Two years later, Tabitha sat down to enjoy a relaxing cup of tea. It was the middle of the afternoon as five children slept in the other room. Kyle, now six, was away at school. Katie enjoyed having other playmates at home all day long, and sure liked her mom staying at home, too.

Tabitha's dream of staying home with her children, teaching young kids, and enjoying healthy finances were all reality. Jack and Tab still owed on their house, yet had no other debts. They continued to communicate as they worked their plan for financial freedom. They enjoyed not having to live paycheck to paycheck anymore.

Word spread quickly of their family's transformation. After Jack and Tab completed their season of financial coaching with Ruth and Ruth's husband, they helped friends and neighbors, such as Linda, who asked for it. They even adapted some of Ruth's material and added their own insights to create their own two-day seminar for married and engaged people, which they titled, "A Couple with Common Cents." Jack and Tab offered this seminar locally and online.

Tab sipped on her tea and sorted through the day's mail. She did not have to worry about the bills. They always had more than enough to cover their expenses.

Tabitha opened the one bill that came that day, wrote out the check, and prepared it for mailing the next day.

She walked to the doorway to check on the sleeping children. Tab looked at these kids each afternoon, and at her family each night, fully aware that she was blessed beyond measure.

STUDY GUIDE

I wrote the following study guide and questions to help you apply the lessons you learned from this story to your own family. You may work together with your spouse or a couples small group as you discuss these.

 # PENNY CHOICES

You make choices every day:

- How fast to drive the car,
- What you eat,
- How much food you put on your plate,
- Whether or not to buy the latest "thing" promoted by commercials or talked about by your friends, and
- Whom you will talk to…and how much you tell them.

These choices may seem small at the moment.

But like pennies, these choices add up, and set the stage for larger decisions you need to make. When you put together all of your seemingly "small" daily choices, you quickly see how they are so integrated into the larger decisions you've made about how you treat yourself and those around you.

When you realize how all your small choices and larger decisions about money affect each person around you, you begin to treat finances differently.

And then, your relationships will improve as well.

Pennies are the foundation of your dollars. In the same way, your daily choices add up to where you are right now.

Worldview

Every day, you live according to how you see the world. You either see it as a world of scarcity, where you have to argue over which side of the pie–and how much of it–is yours.

Or you see it as a world of order, one where a gracious God gives life, hope, and healing to the brokenness that you encounter. A world where abundance is at the core and you have been given much more than you can ask or imagine.

The way you see the world affects your daily decisions and interactions with other people.

And what you believe about your value, the worth of others, and the nature of money all flows from that as well.

Let's face it: Most of us have had a conversation with our spouse that didnt go well. It might not have been outright arguing and yelling, but the result of the talk left a bad feeling in your gut.

And the topic was money.

Hope

You may feel stuck…as if you were the only one dealing with your financial dismay.

You are not alone.

You see, most married people do struggle with finances from time to time. Even Christians.

Newlyweds and newly engaged couples have much to sort through.

My goal in this series is to raise some questions that will help you think through the money issues that may be troubling you right now in your relationship. You will have more clarity as you discuss the topics that follow in the next several days.

As you work through this study guide, please do not put any blame on yourself, your spouse, or your past.

Make the choice to gently talk with your spouse about what is on your heart.

Do not play the blame game or generate any guilt trips along the journey. That will just hinder the outcome even more.

(And if you are single, many of these tips will help you as well.)

May you open your eyes to all that God has already blessed you with in His marvelous Son!

When Only One Spouse Does the Paperwork

The following is a true story.

One husband started a small engine business after his wife got fired from her job. Even though the household income was less than before, this did not change their spending habits.

The wife began to spend themselves tens of thousands of dollars into the hole. She asked for money from others and borrowed money from her children on many occasions to pay the bills. The wife hid these bills from her husband.

She would always sneak out to get the mail every day. One of their sons always wondered why she did this.

One day, this son went out to get the mail and found some credit card bills. He confronted his mom about it, but she swore him to secrecy!

This son was 13 years old at the time.

(How would you feel if your mother swore you to secrecy at age 13?)

More time passed. This son finally got fed up with the situation. He asked his dad, "Why aren't you doing anything about this? Why aren't you checking on the finances? Why aren't you managing this?" The father just replied with excuses.

It wasn't until about 15 years into this nonsense that things began to change. The husband found out about even more stuff that she had been hiding. She had maxed out a couple of credit cards in the process of doing everything she wanted to do.

Finally it snapped in his mind, so he got up and decided to make a difference.

He told his wife flat out, "You have to go get a job to pay off all these bills, because there's no way we're going to be able to pay them off."

He was right; they were going to lose everything if they didn't pay down the debt. Again, we're talking about tens of thousands of credit card debt.

Once the husband started doing the paperwork and counting the money, in conjunction with his wife, they reduced their debt. They've managed to pay off some credit cards.

No longer is she spending money on junk. They have now bought a truck outright, and this couple is in a better financial state.

The son in this story is now an adult. When he told me this story, I just couldn't believe the situation.

Apparently this type of arrangement is more common than I originally thought.

One of you is probably better at keeping records than the other spouse. I get that. Both my wife and I are capable of keeping the records. I'm the one that prefers to do it, and I keep more detailed records, so I'm the one that tracks our money.

When is the last time you discussed your money together? Set aside time to review your records and future cash flow (budget) together.

It's not just about doing paperwork. This is about being a responsible, mature person.

How do you work together as a couple on the household record keeping?

Do you like to keep records yourself, or do you prefer your spouse to do the paperwork?

How often will you intentionally set aside time to discuss your money together? Does it need to be once a week? Once a month? Find a rhythm that works best for you.

Don't wait 15 years to change your situation. Make some progress starting NOW.

THE ROLLER
COASTER OF RISK

As I observe marriage relationships, I find that one spouse likes to take more risks than the other. This is true in my own marriage.

But each spouse also has his and her own ways of taking risks that the other person does not.

Perhaps you love to travel, explore new places, or climb mountains like my wife, Lori. When you take a first glance at us, you might think she's the one prone to more "risk," if you just look at what she likes to talk about or how she drives the car.

Or perhaps you can handle more fiscal risk. You spend money on investments or opportunities that don't have a clear guarantee. There's a huge upside if it goes right, but there's also opportunity for loss.

In your marriage, I would bet that one of you is financially more conservative than the other. One of you likes to save, while the other one spends. One of you will give away all your money, while the other one says, "Slow down!"

Whether you are the one who is able to take more financial risks, or wants to save more money back, this is one area that you need to discuss.

The roller coaster of risk is different from person to person. It also changes over time: as years go by, you may hold on to your money tighter, or let it go easier. This is another good reason to have this discussion with your spouse. Things may have changed since you last talked about how you handle risk.

Here are some questions for you to consider together:

How do each of you handle risk?

Do you understand why the saver likes to save, and the spender likes to spend?

Do you take calculated risks?

How can you reconcile these differences?

# JOINT GENETICS, SEPARATE ACCOUNTS, AND FINANCIAL INFIDELITY

Many couples have separate "his" and "her" checkbooks. They seem to make it work just fine. Each person pays certain bills, or one pays all the bills and the other pays the groceries. Their incomes go into accounts separately, too. As long as each spouse is in the black, they think they're doing fine.

They're dead wrong. It's a very dangerous thing to keep separate bank accounts. When they are not willing to merge their bank accounts, that's a sign that something much deeper is going on in the relationship.

Look, we're not running a joint venture here. This is a MARRIAGE.

Consider this: You're willing to combine a part of each of you to have children, but not willing to combine your bank accounts? That's ridiculous!

Both the husband and wife must be listed on the signature card as account owners for all bank accounts. Both of you need full access to make deposits and withdrawals. Both need administrative rights to the accounts.

If you have a family business involved, yes, the business accounts need to be separate from your household accounts.

Close unnecessary or old accounts and share one checkbook! (Does anyone use checkbooks anymore?) If you have separate accounts, one "his" and one "hers," I say that's a recipe for financial infidelity. Sure leaves room for other problems.

If you merged all your accounts, excellent! If you haven't, I have a few questions for you to discuss together (don't tell me your answers, tell your spouse):

Why do you have separate accounts?

Do you fully trust your spouse with the money you have together?

Does having separate bank accounts put an unnecessary wall between the two of you?

What Did Your Parents Teach You About Money?

Many couples who think their parents raised them in similar ways don't realize how many subtle differences they have in their childhoods until it is time to handle money or raise children.

Allow me to speak from experience.

My wife and I both grew up on family farms in the Midwest. Both sets of parents instilled in us the traditional work ethic of daily chores, frugal spending, and stewardship of resources.

We both appreciate the way we were raised.

We had much in common in our backgrounds, which was a plus when we first met. Lori and I worked through most of the money differences that we had during our engagement.

One major hindrance to healthy finances for you may be that you have not worked out the differences in how you were raised.

Talk about these together:

How did your parents handle money?

What did they usually do with it?

Were your parents frugal, or not?

Did you ever receive an allowance? If so, what did you usually do with it?

Did your parents ever discuss money with you, or did you just imitate their example?

Is your approach to money different from your parents' approach? In what ways?

 A FLASH IN THE PAN

H ave you ever discussed something just one time with a coworker, family member, or friend, and that discussion became "unwritten law" between you from then until now?

Don't you wish you could change that unwritten law?

Sometimes these little rules we put in place within our relationships really do help us keep healthy boundaries, maintain a sense of stability, and provide good expectations.

But at other times, these one-time "flash in the pan" moments later restrict us in ways we did not intend.

For example, as we apply this idea to money and marriage, you may have had one big money discussion with your spouse in the past that was the end-all to financial talk in your household.

Your one-time talk about money became unwritten family law forever.

You feel stuck.

This may be a real sore spot. You might have wounds you don't want to open again.

It might be at the point when you need outside help, such as from a professional marriage counselor.

Remember the story you recently read? Tabitha felt like this, too. When Tabitha and Jack got married, they took care of their financial aspects at that point, then didn't say much more about it until they had Katie and Tabitha went to work.

Then for a long time, Tabitha wanted to improve their situation. She wanted to stay at home with their kids. She wanted Jack to earn more money. She wished that they could get beyond the paycheck to paycheck.

After frustrating conversations, the weekend women's conference, and a few other events, they finally got back on track.

Here's a question for you: Did you have one talk around the time you got married about your money, and that talk "settled the issue" once and for all?

Or are you discussing your finances on a regular basis?

How can you move to the point where you can discuss money without anger, tension, or strife?

You may need professional help in this issue. Perhaps you need to seek out a Dan or a Ruth in your town.

Maybe all you need is a clear resource to show you some next steps to take. Perhaps a workbook, such as *The Four Week Financial Turnaround* by Derek C. Olsen, would help you the most right now.

Feeling good about money is possible.

 # THE SHACKLES OF DEBT

L et me get this on the table right now.

Debt is an enemy to the abundant life that Christ has given us. When we submit to the handcuffs of debt, we become a slave to it.

"The borrower is slave to the lender." Proverbs 22:7

"Leave no debt outstanding to anyone, except to love one another..." Romans 13:8

So many people continue to submit to the bondage of debt. This may be for various reasons.

Perhaps you've always grown up with it and know no other way.

Maybe a series of decisions led you to red figures.

Maybe you're just holding on to a credit card for "emergencies," yet use it for regular monthly stuff anyway.

Or maybe you're trying to keep up with your neighbors and financing every single purchase you make.

Debt is part of personal identity for some people. One man said, "I don't see any reason to pay off the car. I'm just going to get a loan for the next one!" He has resigned to debt and has no motivation to get out.

Debt becomes a point of despair for some. They think that there is no way out. Or, in their minds they say, "I am a person who will always be in debt," which sounds just like, "I am a slave and always will be a slave." They treat it as an illness or disease, and just accept it as part of who they are.

Because so many people have loan payments and no savings, the moment their income is cut off, they panic and then blame others for the situation that they've gotten themselves into.

Debt in our society as a whole has become an issue of identity.

Then there is the motivation to make it a priority to pay the debts off. Many times the issue of debt is minimized in comparison to everything else that people are dealing with. The internal energy to make the decisions to change just isn't there.

Here's the math:

Let's say you have $1,000 on a credit card, and only make the minimum payments on that amount. It would take you more than 12 years and $1,115 in interest to pay off that card, given an 18% annual rate.

That means you are paying $2,115 for a $1,000 purchase! (Don't you think that's a form of slavery?)

Questions to discuss with your spouse:

What is your view of debt?

Do you currently have debts to pay off? If so, what are they? Do you have a plan to get rid of your debt?

Need help breaking through the shackles of your debt? One of the most well-known financial experts today on the issues of money, life, and debt is Dave Ramsey. He has some tremendous resources to help you on his website: daveramsey.com.

Do You Have a
Savings Buffer?

If you stopped receiving all of your income, how long could
you and your family live?

One week?

Two weeks?

One month?

Even though many people have renewed their interest
in personal savings during the past few years, nearly one-
third of Americans have no "rainy day" or "emergency
fund" for themselves, according to the Harris Poll and
Rasmussen Reports.

You never know when your employer may no longer need
your current position, or when uncontrollable conditions (such

as the summer 2012 drought) lead to much lower business revenue. Your child may need an overnight trip to the emergency room. Your car might have to go to the shop for some parts after an unexpected breakdown.

Life happens. We don't plan on these adverse situations. We don't wish for them to come. Yet, we know that tough times do come, so why not set some money aside for later?

Start Your Savings Buffer

If you're just getting started with your savings, it may seem hard to put aside $100 per month at first. Once you've started your habit (no matter what amount it is), it will be easier for you to continue and put away even more in future months.

Put your savings in a place where you can't spend it easily. Don't attach a debit card to that account. Dont keep your savings within your checking account or in a drawer at home—you will be tempted to spend it when its easily accessible!

To kick-start your savings buffer, to start this new habit, you may want to sell some extra things you dont use anymore. Do you have any extra items sitting around that you might list in the classifieds, on Craigslist, or on eBay? List them.

Should you host a big yard sale this spring? Schedule a date. Find some things, big and small, that you can get rid of.

Imagine a life where you have more margin.

What could you do if you had that savings buffer?

Could you relax more with your family?

Get better sleep?

Stop rushing to the bank the moment you get handed a check?

I assure you: you will make better decisions now for you and your family when you have a cushion of cash to use later.

FIRST STEPS TO
GETTING ORGANIZED

S ometimes the best thing to get your financial life in order is simply to get your paperwork organized.

What can you use?

A shoebox is OK if you don't have many pieces of paper. I prefer a way to keep it all organized by month (or quarter).

Hanging file folders with manila folders inside them work great. These folders, plus a cheap crate or tote, will not cost you much to get started.

Keep all of your bank statements, contracts you sign, papers when opening a bank account, and utility receipts. Keep **all** income and expense paperwork that is related to business activities. Keep past tax returns for seven years.

Your filing system will literally save you hours when you have to look up papers later. There were multiple times I had to go back and check an expense, or pull out a receipt from a few months back. I remembered the month when it occurred, so I went to the right folder and easily found the data I needed.

Take a few moments and get your receipts, bills, and other things lined up in a way that helps you process it faster.

Happy organizing!

WHO ARE YOU IN THIS STORY?

Who did you identify with in this story?

Are you like **Tabitha**, trying to figure things out on your own? Frustrated that your family is in a financial mess? Tried to get your spouse to understand your perspective? Not sure what to do next?

Are you a **Jack**, someone who keeps no records and just trusts that you will have money as long as you keep working?

Maybe you are a **Ruth**. You are wise for your age. You do well with your finances, and you like helping other people get their lives back on track. You may even be a financial coach or counselor yourself.

Or perhaps you are a **Dan**, a business owner, a mentor in the workplace, a resource in the local community. You are involved in your employees' lives, and you want to see them succeed.

Are you like **Jack and Tabitha at the end of the story**? You've struggled before, but now your family is headed in the direction of hope.

No matter who you identify with in the story you just read, you have a choice to make.

Will you set this book down and go about your day as normal, unaffected by Tabitha's message for you?

Or will you begin to experience abundant hope in your finances and life?

Your ability to succeed or fail in personal finances has more to do with your mind, emotions, relationships, and daily discipline, than it has to do with your level of formal education.

THE STORY CONTINUES

A Preview of

THE JACK OF ONE TRADE
The Second Book in the *Copper Coin Chronicles* Series

"Jack, wake up! Were almost ready to land!" Tabitha shook her husband to get him up. A flight attendant walked down the aisle to make sure everyone was prepared to land.

"Sir, excuse me, sir, we are preparing to land. Please put your seat in its upright position," she said.

Hearing the unfamiliar voice, Jack came to. "Sorry, ma'am," he said. Jack looked at his wife and gave her a half-eyes-open look as he put his seat up.

Their stomachs immediately hit their throats. All the luggage above them bounced around in their respective compartments. The captain announced over the intercom, "Sorry about that, folks. We have encountered unexpected turbulence. It appears a thunderstorm is brewing up, but well have you on the ground in about 15 minutes."

"Ugh, I don't feel so good!" Katie moaned.

Kyle reached into the seat pocket, tore off the top, and handed his sister the open bag. "Whatever you do, make sure you get it in that bag. I don't want you sick all over me," he said.

"Katie, thats why I told you to not be snacking the whole time were on the plane," her mother said. "I know this is your first time flying, and we have one more fight in front of us—a longer one."

The plane shook a few more minutes before they touched down at Houston.

"I am so glad to be on the ground," Katie said. "I almost spewed everywhere."

"That would've been some way to start our family vacation," her brother said as he rolled his eyes. "Now, give me some space to play my game." Kyle was always doing something on his phone, yet only used it as a phone when his parents called him.

As the Cundiff family walked into the terminal, Tabitha checked the status of their connecting flight to Mexico City. "Were still right on time," she announced. "We have about one hour until we board our next flight. Everyone have their stuff ready?"

"Sure, I think we all do. Thanks for staying so organized, honey," Jack said.

"Just doing what I do best, Jack. Quick, we want to make sure we catch our connection."

As the four of them ran toward the international terminal, the status board for flight 273 to Mexico City changed from on time to delayed.

"What do you mean were delayed?" Kyle said. "The screen said 'On Time' just a few minutes ago!"

The four of them made an extra effort to get to the gate fast. They ran to their gate only to discover that they would have to wait–indefinitely.

"Here we are, trying to get out of here so we can relax, and look at us now, stuck at the airport!" said Kyle.

"I think someone was already getting very relaxed on this trip," Tab said as she glanced over at Jack.

"Yes, I got some great sleep on that first flight. I haven't had time for a nap like that in months. Which is why were taking this trip now, to get a break and enjoy it together. Katie, how are you feeling?"

"I'm feeling better now, Dad, thanks," she replied. "I just wish my brother would hold his horses and calm down."

"We know, sweetheart," her mom said.

"Ladies and gentlemen, can I have your attention please," came a booming voice over the speakers. "Fight 273 to Mexico City is now cancelled…"

Want to read another excerpt from *The Jack of One Trade* and be notified when that book releases? Enter your email on this webpage:

ryaneidson.com/jackpreview

About the Author

 **Ryan Eidson** (pronounced ED-son) has the unique ability to make complex ideas easy to understand as he speaks and writes. He is the founding editor and publisher of *Macon The News* and *The Maple Messenger*, community newspapers based in Macon, Missouri.

Ryan has a wide range of experiences through his work and travel adventures. He and his wife, Lori, grew up on small family farms in the Midwest.

To check out Ryan's blog, or to contact him, **please visit ryaneidson.com**

Printed in the USA
CPSIA information can be obtained
at www.ICGtesting.com
JSHW080000150824
68134JS00020B/2197

9 781630 477127